The Little Book of
CURSES AND
MALEDICTIONS
for Everyday Use

Dawn

Skyhorse Publishing

Skyhorse Publishing books may be purchased in bulk at special discounts for
sales promotion, corporate gifts, fund-raising, or educational purposes. Special
editions can also be created to specifications. For details, contact the Special
Sales Department, Skyhorse Publishing, 307 West 36th Street, 11th Floor,
New York, NY 10018 or info@skyhorsepublishing.com.

Skyhorse® and Skyhorse Publishing® are registered trademarks of Skyhorse
Publishing, Inc.®, a Delaware corporation.

Visit our website at www.skyhorsepublishing.com.

10 9 8

Paperback ISBN: 978-1-62087-190-4

Library of Congress Cataloging-in-Publication Data

Downton, Dawn Rae, 1956-

The little book of curses and maledictions for everyday use /
Dawn Rae Downton.

    p. cm.

ISBN 978-1-62087-190-4 (pbk. : alk. paper)

1. Incantations. 2. Blessing and cursing. I. Title.

BF1558.D69 2009

133.4'4—dc22

                      2009014344

Printed in China

For every evil under the sun
There is a remedy, or there is none.
If there be one, seek till you find it.
If there be none, never mind it.

—Mother Goose

Contents

16
THINGS TO KNOW
BEFORE YOU BEGIN

Take care to read every one of these points below before you start—and then read them again. Before you even consider laying any curse, know all sixteen like the back of your hand. They'll tell you whether you should be considering laying a curse at all. And if they do tell you to go ahead, they'll arm you and protect you when you do.

The bottom line? Take care, and begin that care here. You're dealing with curses, don't forget. It's like working in an ammunition depot!

Why put a curse on someone anyway?

Why not? You've tried everything else. You've asked nicely. You've been patient, willing to compromise. You've been so relentlessly reasonable—and so fed up!—you feel like a pushover. Now you've been shut out altogether. So, try a curse! It's cheaper than a lawsuit and more civilized than punching someone out. (And you probably won't have to explain it to the police.)

I don't know the first thing about it.

You don't need to. Here are custom maledictions for situations you run into every day, for people you know and wish you didn't, even for people and institutions you've never known and never want to. Step-by-step, this book puts control back in your hands. It adapts ancient curses from cultures around the world for your personal use today.

I don't have a goat to sacrifice.

The effects you get with a curse can be powerful, but the ingredients you use are commonplace. Most everything you need is already in your kitchen cupboards, your fridge, your medicine cabinet, your backyard, your garage, your office. All that rubble in your night table drawer? It's a gold mine.

Will it work?

It will if you believe it will—and if you follow the rules below. Did you know that genteel ladies in the Middle Ages scribbled spells and incantations in the margins of their prayer books? They got results, and so can you. But always remember that doing nothing can sometimes turn out to be the best thing to do. Not every problem can be solved. Some battles aren't worth fighting, and the stress can poison you. ("One of the most time-consuming things is to have an enemy," said the writer E. B. White.) Laying a curse shouldn't make you bitter, nor should you be obsessed with its outcome. If you are, you probably won't get what you want. Step back and let your curse work—no monitoring, no fussing, no touch-ups.

There are lots of curses in this book! How do I know which one to use for what?

Easy. There are just four basic types:

THE REVENGE CURSE

When you've been stabbed in the back, nothing else will do. But remember: Betrayals are, unfortunately, pretty common, so pick your battles. Not everything calls for a curse. Know when to walk away.

THE WARNING CURSE
Use it to ward off a betrayal coming down the line.

THE BINDING CURSE
Also known as the neutralizing curse, it ends stalemates, wears down enemies, gets you noticed, and gets your calls returned. Whenever you can, choose a binding curse instead of a revenge curse. In the black art of malediction, less is usually more. Binding spells are gentler and more idiot-proof than revenge curses, and will leave you feeling better in the morning.

THE REPUDIATION CURSE
It guards you from organized malice. Use it against institutions that mislead or hurt people.

To find the one that best suits your purpose, consult the variations the book provides for each curse type. You'll learn which curse to use for what (or whom), how to place it, and what to expect. Some come with incantations, and some even invoke kind but powerful spirits to help you.

Spirits? Yeeks!

Relax. Spirits of one sort or another are around you everyday anyway, and they're awesome. (Literally.) You'd like them (except maybe for that bunch who come dragging chains from the netherworld), and they'd like you, too. More important, if your cause is just, they don't like your enemies.

Is cursing ethical?

This book's methods are karmically and ethically sound. There's even a section on how to place blessings, because sometimes life's like that, too. A caveat, though (and we can't stress this too strongly): Make sure you deserve the remedy you're asking for. Have you truly been harmed by the person or the institution in your sights, or have you instead been hurt by events that have been beyond everyone's control? Try a little self-examination, too. Sometimes, if not frequently, we imagine trouble has beset us from outside, when in fact we've brought it on ourselves. The bottom line is this: If you aim a curse at an innocent, your curse is not ethical and not karmically sound. It's also dangerous to you.

Okay, so I've got a legitimate complaint and I need a curse. How soon can I cast it?

That depends on the kind of curse you're using. Cast a warning curse as soon as you sense a threat coming at you. Don't even wait to know for sure. (If you turn out to be wrong and no one's got you in his sights after all, your warning curse will simply glance off him and won't blow back on you.) But don't be in a hurry to cast a revenge curse. A revenge curse can really hurt, and you don't want to sock it to someone without being sure he deserves it. You also want to be sure you've taken all other steps you can to resolve the problem. Don't take binding and repudiation curses lightly either. Never cast any curse casually, or as an experiment, or when there's time to wait and see what happens by itself.

Is there anyone I shouldn't curse?

Never curse someone who isn't responsible for your trouble! Never cast a curse on someone near and dear to your enemy in order to hurt him vicariously. Never curse yourself, unless it's a self-help "self-curse"—like the one in this book—designed to free you of a bad habit.

Never curse a child or an animal. Don't curse someone who's sick. If you choose to curse a loved one who's hurt you, consider the future. Do you want to lose him or her forever? Lay that curse, and you will.

Can I curse people I don't know who've hurt me? Can I curse institutions or groups?

Yes, and yes. But stay away from the IRS, FBI, NSA, and CIA if you know what's good for you, or unless they've really, really harmed you or harmed your family. (Consider a repudiation curse if you like. You're sheltered there.) Whatever you do, make sure you don't curse innocent people at an institution. Most of them are simply trying to make a living, just like you. Focus instead on whomever's tormenting you. Find out who that is before you start—or curse only the people at the top.

Can I cast a curse on behalf of someone else?

For the most part, no. Never place a curse on behalf of a child. (If your child's been hurt, you've been hurt too, so lay your curse for yourself.) But you can lay a curse on behalf of your family. Never lay a curse for someone who doesn't want payback, protection, or help. Don't make other people's decisions for them.

What if my curse comes back on me?

Everyone worries about this, but you don't need to. Before you embark on a journey of revenge, Confucius said, dig two graves—but he was only partly right. To protect yourself, just follow the rules below. They're not hard to learn. Commit them to memory and follow them exactly. Skip over them or cherry-pick them at your peril.

Sometimes, if you really keep to the rules, you'll find yourself solving your problem some other way. That's always better than resorting to a curse, isn't it? But when a curse truly is in order, here are the rules that will protect you:

- Never try out a curse for a lark. You won't like what happens.
- Ignore the small slights that befall you; they befall us all. It's called life. Curse only when you truly deserve a remedy and can't get it any other way.
- Never cast a curse on someone who's innocent. Never curse someone who *might* be innocent. Wait and see whether he's innocent or not. If you can't cast a curse without causing collateral damage, don't proceed until your enemy becomes an unobstructed target.

- Curse only when your cause is just and true. And remember, you're not always the best judge of who's wronged you and what you're owed.

- Exhaust your options first. Try appeals, entreaties, arbitration, mitigation, and compromise. Jump right to a curse and you'll regret it.

What if someone's innocent when I curse him, and I don't know it? Will my curse boomerang on me?

Make every effort to confirm that the person you want to curse is, in fact, guilty. But accidents do happen. In that case, the curse mightn't "take"—you can hope for it, but you won't know if you've been lucky, at least not immediately. If you've done everything right, including your homework beforehand, the curse normally won't revert back to you—but you won't know that either, at least not for awhile. The best thing to do is nothing. Don't say anything to anyone. Be contrite. But do consult "I changed my mind. How do I remove my curse?" in the FAQs at the end of this book.

Does a curse have a statute of limitations? How long does it last?

That depends on the curse. Some are short; some last centuries; most fade away somewhere in between (and much closer to the short end). Most curses in this book tell you how long they last but if they don't, you can usually decide for yourself. Just specify how long-lived the curse is to be when you lay it. Think long and hard before you stipulate that a curse should last forever, or even for a long time.

Does my victim have to hear my curse to make it work? Does he at least have to know about it?

No, and no. In most cases your "cursee" won't know he's been hit; he'll think it's just a bad flu or a bad patch—or a bad life. Unless otherwise specified, you shouldn't tell him, either. Not ever. Resist the urge to hint, to flaunt it, to say "I told you so," to spit in his face—haven't you already done just that? Really, be an adult about it all. As a general rule, you shouldn't tell anyone that you're casting a curse, or that you already have. Cursing is a lonely art.

What curses won't I find here?

These days we can settle our differences with gentle versions of the ancient maledictions. That means you won't find recipes here to wither crops, sicken livestock, or dry up their milk (or harm any animals at all—and never curse an animal anyway, or we'll send the ASPCA after you. Nine Lives Cat (p. 101) isn't a curse against

11

Fluffy so much as a nudge). Sicko spoiler alert: You won't find incantations here for the complete eradication of anything or anyone. Nothing here will bring on death. (If for no other reason, think of the paperwork!) Neither will we be summoning Lucifer and his entourage, or any dark spirits at all. (Let's just call those netherworld boys "grey.") You can't use this book to disfigure or age your enemy's children, make pregnant women miscarry, make ships hit shoals, or houses catch fire.

These days we don't need to settle our differences by killing people, or turning them into lemmings, or seeing their skin peel off! We don't need to steal their stuff either. Getting back what you're owed is one thing. Just keep in mind that people can be ruined or just plain bothered by many things other than bankruptcy—unless, of course, it's bankruptcy they deserve.

But you will find here the sorts of spells that sour milk; peel paint; shatter china; split seams, zippers, and bra straps; drop pants; and loosen heels inopportunely. You'll find the sorts of spells that make doorbells and car alarms stick at four in the morning; that make dogs eat homework and ink disappear, especially on contracts; that make men impotent and bad employees leave; that break betrothals (or avenge them once they're broken); that make or take money when warranted; and on and on and on. In their way, these were ancient curses too, and they operated side by side with curses that dropped folks dead.

You won't find curses here for the myriad things in life we call "life," the things we all need to "deal with," "let go of," and "just get over"—the guy who cuts you off in traffic, for instance, or any jerk du jour. But the guy who leaves the scene of the accident, the guy who won't pay up, the villain who breaks his word, the claims adjuster who adjusts your claim to zero—these are all fair game.

A word on one more difference between ancient curses and their modern adaptations: As we've said, the intent's the same but the punch is lighter in the modern curse— and often, so are the materials. Many, many old-world curses were cast with elemental, strong ingredients like blood and urine, for example. When you see "wine" (or "sherry") and "stale beer" in these pages, we're really talking about something more basic that's always more powerful than the substitute. Your choice!

And finally, please note: Because spirits can be tricky to handle, spells to invoke them are mostly limited here to a few easy-going types. The ancients called up spirits who were rather more dazzling—and dangerous. We're not doing that here. How're you going to explain it at the ER?

CURSES THEN AND NOW

The Bible speaks of curses, saying a righteous one is more powerful than a godless one. Its first curse is the one God cast on the serpent. Then God cursed the ground, and then Adam and Eve, whom he cast out of the garden. His curse demoted Lucifer to fallen angel. Even today the Roman Catholic church has a place for maledictions, for exorcisms, for purifications. But as part of a global system of religious and cultural beliefs, magic predates Christianity by a long shot. All cultures and all religions use curses—Celts, Hindus, Haitians, Africans and African Americans, Native Americans, Australian Aboriginals, Inuit, East Indians, Occidentals, ancient

Greeks and Romans, Europeans, and Middle Easterners of all kinds. (It's possible that Buddhists, Bahá'ís, and Quakers are the exceptions.) There are even curses in the Qur'an and in the Talmud.

Here are a few famous curses.

The Curse of the Pharaoh

When the boy king Tutankhamen's tomb was opened in Luxor's Valley of the Kings along the Nile in 1922, British newspapers reported something ominous—an inscription near the tomb door that promised "death on swift wings to him that touches the tomb of the Pharaoh." Yikes!

Howard Carter, a British archaeologist, found the tomb's entrance. Typically British, typically unflappable, he raised an eyebrow and carried on. Fifteen feet down into Tut's pyramid, Carter's excavators found a large passageway with stairs. That led to a sealed stone doorway plastered with the pharaoh's seal. That, finally, was enough to make him call for backup: in this case, his underwriter, Lord Carnarvon. At dusk on November 24, both men attended the opening of the sealed door. Two days of rubble-shoveling and another stairway later, they found a second door with more royal seals. Workers cut a hole in it. Carter (who went on to live a long life—you'll be wondering about that by now) looked in by the light of a guttering candle and called back that he could make out "wonderful things," though not Tut's mummy. Getting to that, in the innermost anteroom, took three more dusty months.

Carnarvon—not Carter—opened this inner door on February 17, 1923, only to die forty-eight days later from complications of septicemia that developed when he infected a mosquito bite while shaving. The nurse caring for Carnarvon died promptly as well, and his brother committed suicide. Another team member who'd helped open the mortuary room died early, too, as did curators from the Met and the Louvre. One had helped open the innermost door, and one had visited the inner tomb afterward.

The Kennedy Curse

Everyone knows about the untimely deaths of JFK and RFK. What you might not know is that their oldest sister, misdiagnosed as mentally handicapped, was lobotomized and institutionalized for life. JFK and Jackie suffered a miscarriage; the loss of their first child, a stillborn daughter; and the loss of their last child, a newborn son. Jackie herself died prematurely of lymphoma. Her nephew Edward Jr., son of Ted Kennedy, lost part of his leg to bone cancer at age twelve, and her first son, JFK Jr., died at the controls of his plane along with his new wife and her sister. JFK Jr.'s cousin, Anthony Radziwill, died of cancer just a month later.

JFK's oldest brother and another of his sisters died young in separate air crashes in Europe in the 1940s, and Alexander Onassis, Jackie's stepson, died in a plane crash in 1973. (Some people will tell you the Onassis family has a curse of its own.)

Nineteen sixty nine's Chappaquiddick seems to have repeated itself in 1973 when Joe Kennedy, RFK's oldest, was the driver in a crash that left a woman passenger paralyzed. Another RFK son, Patrick, crashed his car on Capitol Hill in 2006 and went into rehab. He'd been there twenty years earlier for cocaine addiction. RFK Jr. was arrested for heroin possession, and his brother David died of an overdose in a Palm Beach hotel room in 1984. (On the Onassis side, Christina, Jackie's stepdaughter, died a few years later, also as the result of drug abuse.)

And then, the legal troubles. Nearly twenty years ago, a JFK nephew stood a very public date rape trial in Palm Beach; he was acquitted. In 1997, Michael Kennedy,

RFK's son, was accused of adultery and statutory rape and died on the last day of the year in an Aspen skiing accident. Ethel Kennedy's nephew Michael Skakel was convicted in 2002 of murdering a childhood friend when he was a teenager.

Curse 27
You've made it to age twenty-seven? Congrats. Now, run quickly toward twenty-eight. Order your cake and gather your friends ahead of time, especially if you're a musician. For rock stars, that twenty-seventh birthday can be a tough act to follow. Jim Morrison, Jimi Hendrix, Brian Jones, Janis Joplin, Al Wilson of Canned Heat, Ron "Pigpen" McKernan of the Grateful Dead, Gram Parsons, Steve Gaines of Lynyrd Skynyrd, Kurt Cobain—all died at twenty-seven.

The Hope Diamond
Said to be so ill-fated that whoever touches it dies, the Hope is the color of sapphires and the largest blue diamond known. It's been cut and cut again, ending up a broken blue heart. Stolen during the French Revolution, it surfaced in 1830 in England, bought by the London banker Thomas Hope. All his family died in poverty, as did at least one of the stone's subsequent owners.

The blue heart was then bought by the American jeweler Cartier, who caught the society girl Evalyn Walsh's eye with it by telling her it was unlucky. Some folks just can't leave well enough alone, and Evalyn was one. When she married Ned McLean, heir to the *Washington Post*, the couple squandered their families' wedding settlements on the stone, and Evalyn had it blessed. On the way to the blessing service, a tremendous storm blew up, lightning hit the church, and Evalyn's maid fainted. But when the party exited to the street, they met sunshine and calm.

Soon, though, their firstborn was hit by a car and killed. They drowned their sorrows in drink, and Evalyn took up morphine. Headed for bankruptcy, Ned was put into a home and the *Post* was auctioned off. At twenty-four, Evalyn's daughter died of a drug overdose. Evalyn herself died of pneumonia shortly after, and the jeweler Harry Winston bought up her jewels. The Hope left the Walsh estate on a Friday and stayed the weekend with J. Edgar Hoover. (Perhaps he tried it out with a little black dress.)

Harry Winston donated the Hope to the Smithsonian. The man who delivered it had his leg crushed in a traffic accident. Then his wife died young, and his house caught fire.

The Hitler Witches

Making the most of the Nazi high command's belief in the supernatural, Britain's security service, MI5, staged a sorcery ritual in the New Forest in central south England to put the Nazis off their invasion plan. (The site wasn't chosen arbitrarily. New Forest tradition held that the area had been home to an ancient Wicca coven ever since Rufus, a Norman King, died there.) The Witches' Ritual, as it came to be known, was performed on Lammas Eve, 1940, "when the tides and time of year were right" and the moon was in the last days of waning (always an ideal time to get rid of things).

But what none knew but MI5 was that the service was only copying an authentic ceremony that had been staged earlier in the war by real occultists at a site that was also said to be targeted for invasion—the Ashdown Forest in East Sussex.

Across the pond, meanwhile, American witches helped out, too. A 1943 meeting in Greenwich Village that sounds like something out of *Rosemary's Baby* involved a coven of crones knitting, crocheting, and casually casting anti-Nazi spells.

Historians say that just two events stopped the invasion: first, an air campaign of bombings, and then the Führer's unexpected and unexplained change of plan to move east and invade Russia. Was this how the magic manifested?

The Superman Curse

Two thousand six's *Superman Returns* almost didn't get cast. But isn't Superman a role actors die for? Not if the movie's cursed, it seems. Ashton Kutcher turned down the starring role, and Jude Law turned down a supporting role.

The movie almost didn't get made, either. A producer broke ribs in a mugging; the editor fell through a window and punctured a lung; a cameraman fractured his skull and severed a fingertip falling down a flight of stairs. Even Kate Bosworth (the latest Lois Lane) is reported to have said that the Superman curse came between her and longtime love Orlando Bloom.

Casts of the earlier *Superman* movies fared no better. The fates of Christopher Reeve and his wife are the best-known. Reeve's co-star Margot Kidder suffered a nervous breakdown, and Richard Pryor developed MS. Marlon Brando (the Man of Steel's father, Jor-El) had a daughter hang herself and a son jailed for ten years. Lee Quigley, who played the infant Superman in the same production, developed a fondness for sniffing glue and died at the age of fourteen. In the TV series *Smallville* (a *Superman* spin-off), an experienced stuntman suffered multiple fractures and internal injuries in a freak accident. Another stuntman was sliced up when he fell through a window that was supposed to shatter on contact but didn't. Lane Smith, the newspaper boss Perry White in TV's *Lois and Clark* (another spin-off), died suddenly from Lou Gehrig's disease, and Jeph Loeb, who wrote the comics and the *Smallville* series, lost a son to cancer.

Even a Superman-themed rollercoaster may have ridden the Superman curse. The brakes on a Ride of Steel in Massachusetts failed in 2001, injuring several riders, and two other Rides of Steel have suffered catastrophic accidents.

But the curse reaches back further. George Reeves, the Superman of a TV series and several movies in the 1950s, was found dead of a gunshot wound. He was a heavy drinker who'd threatened to kill himself; one night in the midst of a house party he went upstairs and apparently did so. But his prints weren't on the gun, and he'd been having affair with the wife of an MGM exec. These details were ignored or overlooked and the death was ruled a suicide.

Who set the Superman curse in motion? It's attributed to the pair who created the comic book character back in 1938 and sold the rights outright for $130 between them.

The Curse of the Billy Goat

Just one of an impressive volume of curses that explain underperformances, failures, and extraordinary bad luck in sports, the Billy Goat curse concerns the woes of the Chicago Cubs. The team hasn't won a World Series since 1908, and hasn't even reached the series since 1945. It's the longest sports drought in history. What gives?

Billy Sianis, that's what. The Greek immigrant owned a tavern next to Wrigley Field and attended one day with his pet goat, Murphy, for whom he held a ticket for a box seat next to his own. At first, things went well; the game that day was against Detroit, and Murphy paraded the field wearing a coat that read "We Got Detroit's Goat." But then, urged by the field's security head to turn around a losing game by eating his ticket, Murphy declined. It was a slippery slope for a goat, and before long the Cubs' owner had both Sianis and Murphy thrown out.

Sianis answered the insult with his infamous curse. The Cubs lost the game and, eventually, the 1945 World Series. "Who stinks now?" Sianis wrote to Wrigley from Greece, where he'd retired, and where he died in 1970. (No word on the whereabouts of Murphy.)

Sianis's nephew has been brought out on the field repeatedly—complete with a goat—to break the curse, but still it rules. Before he died, Sianis said that in order to lift the curse the Cubs organization had to show a "true, sincere" fondness for goats, inviting them into Wrigley Field because they liked them, not just because they generated publicity.

Sianis liked his own goat a lot, having rescued it when it fell off a truck and limped into his tavern one day. When they were still friends of Wrigley Field, Sianis and Murphy both had season tickets.

Tecumseh's Curse

As the 19th-century Shawnee leader Tecumseh lay dying, he cursed the American presidency: Every president elected in a year divisible by twenty would die in office. The curse is also known as the Presidential Curse, the Zero-Year curse, the Twenty-Year Curse, and especially the Curse of Tippecanoe after the 1811 battle in which President William Henry Harrison defeated Tecumseh and his brother (and chief curse-maker) Tenskwatawa, "the Prophet."

Presidents Harrison, Lincoln, Garfield, McKinley, Harding, FDR, and Kennedy all died according to plan—until Jimmy Carter "escaped" by not winning re-election in 1980, a year divisible by twenty. (Asked about it at a campaign stop before the vote, Carter reportedly said gamely, "I'm not afraid. If I knew it was going to happen, I'd go ahead and be president and do the best I could, for the last day I could.") Ronald Reagan, who did win that year, seemed to escape as well. Reagan *was* shot, though, and survived only because he had immediate onsite care, a modern convenience Tecumseh and Tenskwatawa apparently didn't foresee.

The last president up for the curse? George W. Bush. Oh well.

PERFECTING YOUR TECHNIQUE

Before You Start

A curse is like a recipe. Read and reread it until you understand it. (You don't usually have to memorize invocations. For the most part, it's okay to read them from the book.) Check the "You Need" section at the top and assemble everything before you start. Make sure you're in a quiet place where you won't be interrupted, unless the curse specifies otherwise. When you're ready, take a few moments to focus. Think about what you want to accomplish. Think about what you deserve. If you deserve what the curse promises, and if you deserve to get it from your "cursee," then you can begin.

On Delivery

Be calm and deliberate in your movements and your speech without being stiff. Don't rush. If you get nervous, stop until you're calm again. If you make a mistake, simply go back and correct yourself. If you stumble over your invocations, be sorry, back up, and start again.

On Threes

Most often you'll say and do things three times. As far as cursing methods go, once is almost never enough. Three is a staple of curses and puts your best foot forward. As *The Simpsons* put it, revenge is a dish best served three times. Sometimes spells are triple-cast over a series of three nights, weeks, or months, or at the beginning, middle, and end of a single month.

On Left

Left is the direction and the side of the body (though not the brain) that holds power in casting spells. So you'll generally do things with your left hand, burn documents by beginning at their lower left corner, and so on. When you're instructed to turn, turn counterclockwise (that is, to your left).

On Writing
No pencil, please! Use plain ink, black if you have it. Fountain pen would be lovely.

On Gender
Most curses written to be cast on women can also be cast on men, or vice versa, unless the directions say otherwise.

On Timing
As a general rule, when you want to start something, wait for a new moon. End things under a full one, when the moon begins to wane. According to Nordic tradition, the best spell-casting days of the year are Christmas Day and Midsummer's Day (the June 21 equinox). Don't make strangers of the remaining three equinoxes either. It might be prudent to wait for one or another of them, if you can.

On Candles
Many curses require you to light candles at night in dim light (sometimes in complete darkness) and to snuff

them out when you're through. Flames may gutter when spirits are invoked—or they may not. (Don't worry about it. How your candle behaves signifies nothing whatsoever.) Use the color specified—usually white, but sometimes red. Red candles are the candles of love, though sometimes their use may seem paradoxical. Black candles aren't called for in any spell here because they're next to impossible to find. But if you *can* find them, snap up the lot, and use them when you're doing something splendidly malignant! But never, never use a black candle in a spell involving a relationship, even if it's a relationship you're trying to ruin. Light a candle with a match, never a lighter. Extinguish a flame by pinching the wick between the thumb and third finger of your left hand. Never use your right hand or, worse, a snuffer, and never simply blow out the flame. Your cursing candle isn't a birthday cake! For safety, always set candles in holders or fasten them solidly to small saucers with a little melted wax. (If a candle nevertheless falls in the commission of a malediction, simply stop, set it right, and pick up where you left off. If you invoked a spirit, then singed him and splattered him with hot wax, by all means apologize to him.) Never leave a candle burning when you're finished. Unless a spell specifies otherwise, you can reuse your candles for magic, but not for household use. Keep your candle drawers separate.

On Setting

Casting curses usually means privacy, quiet, and often darkness. Do we need to tell you to turn off the TV? Unplug land lines; turn off cell phones and BlackBerrys. Turn off desktops; close laptops and notebooks. If there are stuffed animals or figurines in the room, turn their faces to the wall. Turn photographs in frames face down. Stow clocks and mirrors. Face large mirrors to the wall. If you can't, lay your curse in another location. Never use magic when a mirror's watching you. Having books around is fine. Except for this one, just make sure they're not lying open. It's fine to consult other books about magic, but have only one open at a time. Rid the room of cameras and of cell phones that take pictures. Under no circumstances photograph or allow yourself to be photographed (or videotaped or filmed or Skyped or anything else), and never record yourself or allow yourself to be recorded. Ignore these guidelines—some are warnings, in fact—at your peril.

On Knots

Here and there a spell might ask you to make a talisman from a hand-tied knot. (If knots aren't your thing, chill—only one spell in this book uses a knot, and it's a simple one at that.) If you need to, practice tying a specified knot before you begin your spell. Never ask someone to tie it for you! When you're finished, don't untie it unless you're told to and don't reuse it. Unless a spell says otherwise, never discard it, either, and never give it away. If you're told to keep it, it's your talisman, so store it in a safe place. If you need a knot for another spell, start with new twine and make a new knot.

On Burials

There's a lot of burying in this book! That's because many curses end by separating you permanently from what you've cursed or, conversely, they want to keep you near a protective totem. Sometimes you bury stuff far away; sometimes you bury it close by. Just follow directions! If you live in an apartment and don't have a yard, use any piece of ground, close by or far away—whatever's required. If you're using public ground, do your burying discreetly. If you're keeping something nearby, you still need a little separation from it. So don't tuck things into flower pots on your balcony, and especially not into house plants (unless specified). Occasionally a curse will call for a burial in freshly turned earth. If that's the case, prepare your spot a day or two before. Never bury anything in a grave.

On Summoning Spirits

Relax! Some curses in this book call in spirits to help. So what? They'll come when called. Other than the instructions you'll use to call them (these vary from curse to curse and are spelled out exactly), that's all you need to know. Don't worry about how spirits manifest, or appear to you, either—or even *if* they appear to you. Whether you notice them usually depends on many things perhaps having to do with you and perhaps with the spirit. (How calm are you? How receptive? And as for the spirit, have you called one who likes to get around, perhaps even do a little shopping while she's out, or have you coaxed out an introvert?) Keep your attention on your curse. Spirits can take care of themselves.

On Saying Spirit Names

Like anyone else, spirits mind if you get their names wrong. Except for names that sound just like they're spelled, pronunciations are provided for any curse here that summons a spirit. Remember, practice makes perfect.

On Discharging Spirits

Don't forget to tell them they're free to go, and thank them for coming and for their help—whether or not you've seen them or felt them, and whether or not you think they've been helpful. (But remember, if you doubt your malediction, and if you doubt your spirit, your magic won't work.) If you do forget to discharge spirits, they'll hang around all night, perplexed, disoriented, and not a little miffed, especially if *Ghost Whisperer* or *The Medium* is on (they're not fans) and *American Idol* or *The Mentalist* is not. It's simple, really. Suspended spirits would rather just go home.

On Privacy

He who tells destroys his spells. Don't tell anyone that you plan to cast a curse, or that you've cast one. Obviously, if you need a friend's help in casting a curse, he must be the closest and most trusted of friends, and you'll have to tell him what's up. Ensure that he'll keep it a secret, too.

What You Do Afterward

Nothing. Do absolutely nothing other than get on with your own life. Step back. Leave your curse alone to do its work. Don't fuss. Don't check to see how well it's working. Especially don't try a "booster" curse.

The Curses

GENERIC REVENGE CURSES
Three Little Curses For Every Payback Purpose

So many betrayals, so little time. Custom curses are always better than generic ones, but what if you're in a hurry? Or what if you just can't decide what will work best? Try one of these no-fuss, one-size-fits-most paybacks.

The All-Purpose Payback
A no-brainer curse . . . literally.

Choose the All-Purpose Payback when you want to "do unto others as they did unto you." It's a *quid pro quo* that will directly return to your oppressor the harm he's caused you. That's why it uses a figurine: it represents your "cursee." That's also why you can't use the All-Purpose Payback when you're feeling put upon generally or when things aren't working out, and "someone's got to pay." Have in mind someone or something specific whom you're paying back. Have in mind as well what he did to you, and focus on sending it straight back to him.

You need:
+ A white candle
+ A small saucepan
+ A long match (a fireplace match is good)

Wait until dark. Melt a candle in the saucepan over low heat.

Remove the saucepan from the heat and wait until the wax is cool enough to handle. Shape it into a rudimentary figurine, working quickly so that you're done sculpting before the wax starts to harden.

Strike the match under the ends of the figurine, first the feet and then the head, and drip them into the saucepan. You don't need to melt them much. As you do, slowly say your victim's name three times.

Extinguish the match between the thumb and third finger of your left hand.

Dispose of what's left of the figurine by burying it in the ground. Replace the soil, level it, and dispose of the wax in the saucepan by reheating it to melting and pouring it on top of the soil.

Your oppressor is now at your mercy just as you were once at his, and in exactly the same way.

The Spite n' Smite
Burn, baby, burn.

This is one of the simplest curses in this book, so use it instead of the All-Purpose Payback (p. 37) when time is of the essence and you want to cut corners. It's better than the All-Purpose Payback, too, when you want to harm your opponent but not necessarily in the exact manner he harmed you, or to the same degree. The Spite n' Smite is good for inflicting a general state of misery. While its initial effects are immediately obvious, its full force takes a little time to reveal itself. Be patient.

You need:

+ A white candle
+ A match
+ A small piece of unlined paper
+ A pen
+ A No. 10 (legal size) envelope

Wait until dark. Light the candle. Write your enemy's name at the center of the paper. Fold the paper in thirds and seal it in the envelope.

Fold the envelope in thirds and pass it quickly through the flame; don't let it catch fire.

Unfold the envelope and again pass it quickly through the flame.

Fold it in thirds once more; again, pass it through the flame.

Extinguish the flame between the thumb and third finger of your left hand.

Go outside and bury the envelope in the ground.

From now on, your opponent will feel really hot and bothered by just about everything. It's no way to live, and sooner or later he'll burn himself out.

Vengeance 3.0
A "third-generation" retribution curse

Ever feel like you're being stalked by a black cloud? Know someone who deserves it more than you—whoever attached it to you in the first place, for instance? Here's a quick and easy curse that yields big results for almost no effort. Your intended recipient doesn't need to be in sight, or even close. You can transfer your cloud straight around the planet if you like. Send it anywhere it's deserved!

 You need:

+ A sewing needle

Stand outside. Good weather's fine. You don't need actual clouds, black or otherwise, but if they're there, that's fine too. Bad weather's not so good, especially if it's raining and you're standing under an umbrella—the umbrella will block the curse. A private spot outdoors is best, but if you have to you can even cast the 3.0 in a crowd.

With the needle, prick the middle finger of your left hand. (Be gentle!)

Aim your finger straight up at the sky and turn around slowly, so that you end up facing the other way.

Quietly, say the name of the person to whom you're transferring your cloud. Slowly lower your arm while repeating the name.

Cradle your left hand in your right and squeeze your hands together the last time you say the name.

That little black cloud now belongs to its rightful owner.

CUSTOM REVENGE CURSES
The Ultimate Malediction

Most curses have always been revenge curses, and they still are. That's why this book has more of them than any other. Look through them when you have time to choose carefully: No curse—especially no vengeance curse—should be cast quickly and thoughtlessly. Considered vengeance is one thing. Casual vengeance is quite another.

Return to Sender
You've been fired—get your job back

Getting back at someone who's harmed you is one thing. Returning things to where they were is quite another. Here you're doing both, so call in the spirit Iao ("Yow") for maximum firepower. He doesn't much like bosses of any kind and will be happy to help. Return to Sender is a binding curse to get revenge on those who fired you, since you get your job back while they wanted you gone. But don't use it if you've been laid off or "made redundant," unless you know that whatever they called it, you really were fired—and through no fault of your own.

You need:

+ A candle
+ A match
+ Your pink slip (if you don't have one, use your last pay stub. If you don't have that either, write "FIRED" on a blank page)
+ An ashtray or a saucer

At night, in darkness, light the candle. Step back, but watch the flame. Say: "*Thundering and lightning-wielding Iao, come.*"

The flame will gutter and lengthen. Without minding what the flame does once you speak, say: "*Thundering and lightning-wielding Iao, cast down, bind, bind together* [say your boss's name here], *the greengrocer whom Himera bore in her womb, he who stays in the neighborhood of* [say your workplace address here]. *Just as you cast down the chariot of Pharaoh, so cast down his soul, his choice, his measure. O Iao, cast him down and shore me up.*"

Hold your letter or pay stub in your left hand. Light its bottom left corner in the flame. Hold it over the ashtray. While it burns and the ashes drop, say: "*Thundering and lightning-wielding Iao, just as you choked the firstborn of Egypt, so choke up his ruling. Now, too, bind, bind down, bind together his ruling, let it overturn, let it fall apart, let it stay and stop from this hour and this day forth.*"

Carefully, let your letter burn completely. When the ashes are cool, tent your hands over them to cover them. Say: "*Now, now, now.*"

Snuff the candle with your thumb and third finger of your left hand. Say: "*Quickly, quickly, quickly.*"

Thank Iao and discharge him.

Bury the ashes in the nearest bit of ground to your workplace that you can find. For privacy, wait until dark the next night. If you can't get close to your workplace, try to find a distant patch of ground. If you know where your boss lives, bury the ashes near his home. But near your workplace is best. Don't dump them in a garbage can inside or a dumpster outside, since they'll be transported from there to a place you haven't chosen. You don't want them ending up in a dump, mixed with unthinkables! You want them to stay where you put them. Keeping control over these ashes and leaving them alone is key to the curse.

When you get your job back, don't point out the burial place to anyone or tell anyone about it. Don't go and check on it, either.

The Flush-a-Bye
You've been fired—get your boss fired too

This curse is adapted from an ancient Thailand, where the Thais sealed a possession or a likeness of an oppressor into a clay pot and threw it into a fast-running river, never to be seen again and eventually to be smashed and destroyed upon the river rocks. (Ancient as it is, the curse was revived briefly in honor of George W. Bush when he visited the country in the midst of a Thai-U.S. trade dispute.) Don't use the Flush-a-Bye if you've been "laid off" or "made redundant" unless you know that whatever it was called, you really were fired through no fault of your own. Only use it on the person or people responsible. Find out who that is. It might not be your boss at all; it might be *his* boss.

You need:

+ Scissors

+ A picture of your boss (why not snap it on your cell as you leave, and give him something to think about? If you can't get a picture, get a possession—something small of no value, like a paperclip from his desk)

+ A pint of flat beer (remember: to maximize magic, you do what you have to do)

48

Cut the picture into nine pieces—three if the picture is really small. If you're using something belonging to your boss, break it into three bits.

Overnight, soak the bits in your marinade. (Do you need gloves?) In the morning, fish out the bits and flush them down the toilet with a marinade chaser. Say: "*Bye-bye boss, bye-bye boss, bye-bye boss.*"

Flush twice again, repeating the incantation each time. Rinse those gloves!

Hex-Your-Ex
You've been dumped—get revenge on your ex

This is a nasty curse. Do you really want to cast it on someone you once loved? Engraved in haphazard Latin on a small metal disk, it came out of the southern Italian city of Minturno, and was probably scratched off in haste. But don't be hasty now. Hex-Your-Ex is the rare curse that can inspire karmic backlash. There's no way to remove it, either; and to make things worse, you're invoking netherworld spirits. They can be a bit touchy, so take care. You won't find them in Disney World.

You need:

+ Some small possession your ex left (clothing, a note, a hair from a hairbrush)
+ A short length of twine
+ A square of black cloth

Choose a private spot where you can dispose of your ex's belonging by burying it or throwing it in a river (not the ocean where it might wash back up on shore). No garbage cans; no dumpsters either. It needs to stay where you put it.

Arrive at dusk. Using the twine, tie up your item in the cloth. Dispose of it.

Make three counterclockwise turns on or near the spot and say: "*Spirits of the underworld, I consecrate to you* [say your ex's name here]. *Whatever she does, may it all turn out wrong. Spirits of the netherworld, I consecrate to you her limbs, her head, her hair, her brain, her forehead, her eyebrows, her mouth, her nose, her chin, her cheeks, her lips, her speech, her breath, her neck, her liver, her shoulders, her heart, her lungs, her chest, her breasts, her fingers, her hands, her navel, her entrails, her groin, her knees, her heels, her soles, her toes. Spirits of the underworld, I consecrate and hand over to you her shadow in addition.*"

Thank the spirits politely—don't forget—and discharge them. Leave and don't look back.

The Homewrecker
You want to destroy a marriage

Do you really? Well, here's an old Roman-Gallic spell, not much changed, that sours two paired souls. Small problem: if they're innocent souls, you'll sour your own as well. Homewrecker looks like simple voodoo but it's not. It's even nastier than Hex-Your-Ex (p. 50) and can also cause karmic backlash. If you grow contrite or fearful after casting it, try to remove it. See Cursing FAQs (p. 152) as well as the custom antidote below—and good luck; you'll need it. If you're motivated by fear, not remorse, or if you wait too late, you'll find backing out of any curse, especially this one, next to impossible.

You need:

+ Two 12 x 12-inch squares of cloth (you can cut cotton dishtowels)
+ A bag of cotton balls
+ Twine
+ Five hat pins or other large dressmaking pins
+ A really sick mind

Fashion two rudimentary dolls from the dish towels, cutting them to size and stuffing them with cotton balls. Tie them with twine to make heads and limbs. Tie them together face to face in an embrace. Drive pins through the heads, the chests, the abdomens, the legs, and the feet, in that order. Say: "*You'll not have an hour of bliss. You'll not have an hour of death.*" Bury the dolls, still tied together, in freshly turned earth, and never disturb them.

To reverse the spell, try unburying the dolls. Don't untie them. Shake them free of all soil, coat them in salt—lots of salt—and wrap them in a clean white cloth. Dig a trench around the hole where they lay and set them back in the hole. Burn them to ashes. When they're cool enough to touch, scoop out half the ashes and scatter them all along the trench. Leave the rest of the ashes in the hole. Cover everything with soil and smooth it out. Say: "*Together, you have your bliss. Together, you have your death.*" Walk away without looking back.

The Perp Walk
Curse for the credit crunch No. 1

This simple, elegant warning reminds your financial institutions of the agreement they made, once upon a time, to grow your money, and it reminds them rather publicly. Kindly spirits abhor malfeasance, and so the Perp Walk calls on the spirit world's kindest. They're "unionized" into a task force of Spirits General, "the Kings, Dukes, Governors, and Commanders of the legions for the gathering of the forces to a single will," according to an ancient text. Cast this spell only correctively: "No frivolous call, this summons should only be performed when the importance of the need is such as to not bring wrath and retribution upon ye." In other words, don't use it to try to make money you didn't have to begin with. Don't even use it to try to get your own money back. (Like that's going to happen anyway.) Simply get the Spirits General into each of your financial institutions: your bank, your mortgage holder (if you still have one), your brokerage firm.

You need:

+ Your account numbers

+ A pen

+ This symbol, for summoning the Spirits General:

Visit each of your institutions. Pick up a blank transaction slip. Anything will do. Simply try to find something that bears the institution's logo or letterhead.

Print your account number on the slip, anywhere at all, and then somewhere on the margin casually draw the Spirits General symbol and print "SPIRITS GENERAL" next to it. If this doesn't fit on the margin, turn the slip over and use the back.

Leave the slip anywhere. You can even drop it in a wastebasket. Wherever you put it, it'll find its way into the shredder eventually—but the spirits will be in and off to the races. Bet on it.

Thank them and discharge them.

Walk away and don't look back—itself a fine principle to follow when it comes to any loss.

Break Your Brokers
Curse for the credit crunch No. 2

So you can't get your money back? Make it so they can't, either. The great power of this curse is inversely proportional to its wonderful simplicity.

You need:

+ A pen
+ Paper
+ A stamp
+ This symbol for summoning the Spirits General, your go-to guys in the credit crunch (see the Perp Walk, p. 54):

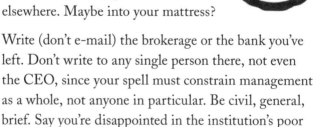

Move what's left of your investments elsewhere. Maybe into your mattress?

Write (don't e-mail) the brokerage or the bank you've left. Don't write to any single person there, not even the CEO, since your spell must constrain management as a whole, not anyone in particular. Be civil, general, brief. Say you're disappointed in the institution's poor judgment, or something like that.

Sign your name; add your address; make this look like a real complaint.

Now, the *pièce de résistance*. On the letter itself (not the envelope—you want it to get there!) spell the institution's name backward. "Dear AIG" becomes "Dear GIA"; "Lehman Bros" becomes "Sorb Namhel."

Thank the Spirits General and discharge them.

Mail your letter.

Sit back and watch the brokerage's executives hand back or be denied their bonuses.

The Stopwatch
You've been stiffed

For investment losses, don't use the Stopwatch. Instead, use the Perp Walk (p. 54) or Break Your Brokers (p. 56). Use the Stopwatch when "your check is in the mail"—when you've been promised money or a payment that you didn't get.

You'll need:

+ A winding watch from a dime store (not digital or self-winding or battery-powered. Look for a child's watch if necessary)
+ A No. 10 (legal size) envelope
+ A pen

Do up the watch strap. Wait until the watch runs down. Set it to twelve o'clock. Don't wind it. On the envelope, write the name you want to curse. Seal the watch inside.

Deliver it—or get it as close as you can. Leave it with a doorman, on a doorstep, in a mailbox, at your debtor's place of work. If it's a store or a business that's stiffed you, drop the envelope somewhere on the premises where it won't immediately be seen. (A wastebasket is fine.) If necessary, mail the watch, but for that you'll need to seal it into a sturdier envelope.

You may or may not get your money. But your victim's fortunes will now stand still, whether or not he finds the watch and whether or not he disposes of it.

Pollard
You've been robbed

Pollard's long ingredient list and the five or so days it takes to cast are all well worth the trouble because this curse yields great results. It gets its name from a legendary English blackguard for whom it was first devised. Use it to retrieve anything that's been stolen from you—your property, your health, your work, even your identity—while your thief forfeits his. You can use Pollard to retrieve investment losses if your broker has defrauded you (as fraud is defined under the law), but don't generally use it for investment losses. Instead, use the Perp Walk (p. 54) or Break your Brokers (p. 56).

You need:

+ A necklace or (for men) a chain
+ A handful of mint leaves (supermarkets sell fresh herbs year-round—don't use dried)
+ A spoon
+ A small glass jar with a lid
+ Table salt
+ Sweet red wine or sherry, about a cup
+ A fine-meshed strainer

+ A coffee or spice grinder
+ A small cloth pouch
+ A flat round stone measuring 3 inches across, or more
+ Drawing graphite (an ordinary pencil will do in a pinch)
+ A timer or a watch with a second hand

Put on the necklace or the chain, and wear it throughout the casting of Pollard.

Pull the mint leaves from the stems. Discard the stems and crush the leaves with the back of a spoon. (Don't tear or chop them.) Place them in the jar with three pinches of salt; cover with wine and swirl to mix. Cover tightly and set in a dark cupboard for three days.

After three days, strain. Return the tea to the jar and return the jar to the dark closet. This is your potion, and it's potent. Keep it out of reach of children and pets.

Dry the leaves for two days on paper towels, then grind them up and place them in the cloth pouch. This is a protective amulet of great power. Keep it in a safe place for whenever you need it.

On the stone, with the graphite, write the name of the person or outfit who's stolen from you. If you don't know the name, write "POLLARD."

Retrieve the jar from the closet. Remove your necklace or chain and place it in the tea for precisely three minutes. (Use the timer or the watch.) Put it back on while it's still wet.

Take the stone and the tea outside, or place the stone in a sink. Pour the tea over it. Lay your hands on it and say slowly and quietly: *"Unto me what is mine. Unto me what is mine. Unto me what is mine. Unto me what is yours. Unto me what is yours. Unto me what is yours."*

And it will be. And the stone? Just throw it away.

The Graverobber
You're out of the will

Think it's a long shot to curse the dead, or at least redundant? You're wrong. The ancient Greeks, for instance, specialized in restraining the ghosts of the dead by building small effigies called poppets for the purpose. (Poppets and voodoo dolls? Same, but different. Voodoo works on the living—or some manifestation of them. Poppets mess with the already-dead.)

The Greeks not only bent and bound their poppets, they tore them limb from limb, pierced them with spikes and needles, bent the heads to ensure eternal confusion, or hacked heads off altogether so that they couldn't rejoin bodies and revive.

None of that here, please. Play nice.

The Graverobber probably won't win you a jackpot, sorry. But it is a great leveler. Before you cast it, make sure your dead guy was indeed the one who willfully disinherited you, not someone who influenced or took advantage of him, or simply made a mistake. Make sure your exclusion was unjustified, too. Were you a good nephew? Did you visit?

You need:

+ A possession of the deceased (believe it or not, a shoe is best. If you can't find a shoe, use a slipper or a sock; whatever you can find. It has to be pliable because you're going to bend it)
+ A good length of heavy twine

Take the shoe and bend it heel to toe, then wrap enough twine tightly around it that it's bound as bent. You're restraining a ghost and canceling the effect of a will.

Say: "*I hereby bind* [deceased's name here]. *May* [name] *be defeated; may* [name] *be restrained. May* [name] *be restrained in hand and foot and head and heart. May* [name] *be disappointed in all intention.*"

Set the bound shoe on the deceased's grave at dusk. (Have someone you trust do this for you if the grave is at a distance; if, say, you're in New York and the grave's in Los Angeles.)

Say: "*Cold and powerless is* [name]*; cold and powerless is* [name] *in thought and effect.* [Name's] *soul, his mind, his tongue, his plans, let all these things be twisted now.*"

Leave the shoe atop the grave and walk away without looking back.

The will's effect is now bound. The ghost may be a little ticked, too.

The Promise Keeper
You've been had

Not much power is used here, but a lot is generated. He's lied to you, so reel him in . . . and then cut him off at the knees. That's pretty well what he did to you, isn't it? To invoke the spirit or a soul of an enemy who disappoints, Promise Keeper uses a pentagram (a five-pointed star shape long used in magic) and mace (a spice ground from the lacy red shell of the nutmeg seed). Mace costs much more than nutmeg and works a lot harder. In a pinch you can use nutmeg, but be prepared to use a lot more for lesser results.

You need:

+ A 1/2 cup of ground mace (available in the spice section of any grocery store)
+ A small, clean squeeze bottle or a clean container with a narrow spout (a lidded baby's cup, for instance)
+ Five fresh oak leaves
+ Five candles
+ A match

Put the mace in the squeeze bottle.

In a dim room, spread the oak leaves on a table with stem ends together and points out so that they form a rudimentary pentagram. Place a candle at the point of each leaf.

Carefully squeeze or shake out the mace and scatter it in a closed circle outside the candles. Make a thin, tidy line, and get it right the first time—you can't patch it up because you can't touch the mace until the spell is complete. (Break a circle; break a spell.) Use a little more mace if that's what it takes to close the circle. It will contain the soul you evoke and prevent it from escaping.

Light each candle, beginning with the one at the head and then moving clockwise. As you light the candles around the circle, say: "[Name of betrayer here], *I summon you here so that you may attend my desire as you once did not.* [Name], *I summon you here in the power of the everlasting virtue of the highest that I attend and you did not.* [Name], *thy skill I desire so to honor me justly. Let this pass between us. Grant me your skill. Suffer the pain of your disregard.*"

Hold your left hand next to the first candle and get ready to snuff it. Say three times: "*So this I ask. So let this be. So will this be.*" Snuff the first candle.

Working counterclockwise, repeat one by one with the other four, intoning the three phrases three times and then extinguishing the flame with your left hand.

Brush up the leaves together with the mace and take it all outside. Roll up the leaves and bury them in freshly turned soil; scatter with the mace.

The Book Curse
Your work has been stolen

Unimaginable but true: Writers in the Middle Ages somehow got by without 128-bit encryption, firewalls, date-stamping, caches, and passwords. Plagiarism was a breeze—and so a scribe (the writer's secretary) might occasionally heed the call of a life of crime. Enter the Book Curse, with penalties harsh enough (excommunication, damnation) to deter theft and the defiling of manuscripts, every one of which was considered precious back then. (Talk about unimaginable!)

But honest scribes far outnumbered maliciously ambitious ones, and "for the honor, protection, and great good" of his master, the noble scribe might write a preemptive curse in a manuscript's colophon (designated white space on the page which was the scribe's to use as he liked). Colophon curses are plentiful, unique, creative, even flamboyant. Folios might clamp themselves on a thief's hand like a manacle, for instance; or scripted words might madden or blind him.

Originating from the San Pedro monastery in Barcelona, the Book Curse that follows is not so bad as that, depending on how you feel about poisonous snakes. While you can't use it preemptively as the medieval scribes did, you can use it to recover your work.

You need:

+ A white candle

Wait until dark. Memorize the incantation if you can. Light a white candle, stare at the flame, and chant three times: "*For him that steals or borrows and returns not this work from its owner, let it change into a serpent in his hand and rend him. Let him be struck with palsy and all his members blasted. Let him cry for mercy and let no mercy come. Let there be no surcease till he cry in dissolution, and then let the serpent pass between us into my hand where as my work it changes back and sings.*" Extinguish the candle.

The Letter
You've been framed

This is an ancient curse whose origins have been lost. It's from a very old school of magic where simplicity was thought to wield more power than ornamentation (and where ornamentation was almost unknown). Many scholars of charms and curses today agree that less is more, and many, likewise, have a preference for really old curses. That doesn't mean you have to, but if you need to assert your innocence and expose a deception, try the Letter. It once used torn vellum, but now paper's fine.

You need:

+ Paper
+ A pen
+ An envelope

Fold the paper in half, crease it sharply, and tear it in two. Arrange the pieces side by side with the torn edges together. Write your name in the middle of the piece on the right. Write the name of the person who framed you on the left. (If you don't know who framed you, write "NOT ME.")

Exchange the pieces so that your name is now on the left, the other name is on the right, and the torn edges are no longer together. The mismatched edges represent your separation from your enemy and the power he had over you. The exchange of name placements returns you to the left, in the position of power.

Seal both pieces in an envelope with your piece on top. Take care that the edges of the two pieces stay mismatched. Keep the envelope nearby in a safe place until your fortunes are reversed and your enemy exposed. It's a hard-won talisman for you, so even then don't throw it out.

Pocket Change
You're collateral damage

Maybe you're caught in an office shake-up or a domestic shake-down that doesn't involve you. Innocent bystanders can use Pocket Change (literally!) to escape. It comes from an Old Norse spell that ransomed beloved children, treasured pets, and valuable livestock from Rae, a wood devil who claimed ownership of anyone and anything he found wandering, lost, in "his" Old Norse woodlands. But Rae was locked in eternal battle with the god of the forest who protected the lost. This good god was sleepy *skogsraet* ("skoogsreut"), the forest's guardian spirit. The spell bound Rae by invoking *skogsraet*, who was ultimately stronger. But *skogsraet*, being an ancient spirit, nodded off a lot, and he had to be roused before he started saving anything. Bereaved families threw coins into the forest for both purposes—to bribe Rae and to wake *skogsraet*.

 You need:

+ An odd number of coins (you don't need many. No subway tokens, please.)

Put your coins in a left-hand pocket and carry them to the woods—a park, a green space, a forest. A forest is best, though any green space will do. Three trees is an absolute minimum, and even then you're stretching it. The more trees you can find in one place, the better.

Go when it's dark and no one is around. Stand within the trees. If there aren't many trees, stand in front of them. With your right hand, throw your coins over your left shoulder into the trees. Thank both spirits (yes, Rae gets thanked too, believe it or not), discharge Rae, invite *skogsraet* to go back to sleep, and leave your change behind.

The Figure Eight
You didn't get what you paid for

Many charms separate you from the thing that promises
danger or inflicts harm, but this one ties you again
to what you're owed. It's meant to be a gentle curse,
so if you've been defrauded, use a nastier one instead.
Retrieving what was yours, or what you're owed,
is one thing. But never use this curse to steal from
someone. (Never use *any* curse to steal from someone!)

 You need:

+ A white candle

+ A match

+ A short length of twine

+ You'll need to know how to tie a figure-eight knot (a figure
  eight is simple to tie: see below. But if knots aren't your
  thing, practice tying a couple before you begin).

In a darkened room, light the candle. With the twine, tie a figure-eight knot or (if you know how to tie knots) a more complicated knot, though it must be one that tightens rather than slips apart when pulled at each end.

Pull the knot tight and say: *"As these threads I do entwine, let your wealth be linked with mine."* Extinguish the candle.

Sleep with the knot under your pillow for three weeks; after that, keep it in a safe place. Never give it away, and never throw it out.

The Slinky
You lost the job

So you lost. Whistle a happy tune anyway—an innocent little tune that you stick in your victor's head to
the exclusion of all else: While he's "on Slinky," he'll
sound incoherent. Use Slinky to unseat someone to
whom you lost a job, a promotion, a contract, or a part
you auditioned for; even an arbitration or a court deci-
sion. Or simply sock it to the jerk who barged ahead
of you in line or stole your parking spot. (See also the
Eastwood, p. 93.)

You need:

+ The Slinky Song!

What walks down stairs, alone or in pairs
Making a slinkity sound?
A spring, a spring, it's a marvelous thing
Everyone knows it's Slinky!
It's Slinky, it's Slinky, for fun it's a wonderful toy
It's Slinky, it's Slinky, it's fun for a girl and a boy
Everyone knows it's Slinky!

Go to the office, or wherever it was you were bested. Cue Slinky in your head, congratulate your victor and shake his hand warmly—and imagine Slinky "slinking" out of your hand and into his. If you see it, it will go— and so will he—on sick leave while he gets his head examined.

Debugging No. 1
You've caught a bug

For use against common STDs, Debugging No. 1 assumes you know who infected you, and it assumes that person is someone you never want to see again. If you don't know who infected you, or if you were infected by someone who's not to blame, use Debugging No. 2 (p. 112). Use Debugging No. 1 and No. 2 along with whatever remedy your doctor recommends—don't use them as a substitute for medical treatment.

 You need:

+ Ingredients for Pollard (p. 60) steps 2 to 6
+ A small saucepan
+ A tablespoon measure and a teaspoon measure (neither can be plastic)

Make the dried mint and steep the tea as per Pollard steps 2 to 5.

Make the cloth pouch as per Pollard step 6.

In the saucepan, heat a tablespoonful of the tea to scalding. Cool it a little. Stir in a teaspoonful of the mint, and drink.

Fill the pouch with the leftover mint and take it to the home of the person who infected you. Sprinkle a little mint over or near his doorstep.

Next, approach him at your earliest opportunity. Walk three times around him, sprinkling most of the rest of the mint. Move quickly; leave quickly; say nothing.

Cast the rest of the mint to the wind—don't keep it for another use.

Do keep the cloth pouch. Store it with the potion in a dark, safe place. Keep it out of reach of children and pets.

Cats will like your victim from then on, but prospective dates will not.

Stardust
You're losing

It's a battleground out there. It seems like everyone's getting ahead while you're not. The Elizabethans had a nice curse for their enemies at times like these: "May you be a candle on the stone," they'd leer, "to hang by day and die by night." But you don't need to vanquish others to feel you're in step with them. Use Stardust instead.

You need:
+ A whole chicken frame left over from soup or from a store-bought rotisserie bird
+ A resealable freezer bag
+ A mallet or meat tenderizer
+ A sieve
+ A small cloth pouch

Dry the bones completely over several days. Seal them in the freezer bag and pulverize them with the mallet. Sieve, reserving the fine stuff. Dispose of the rest.

Be patient and wait for a new moon, when natural cycles renew themselves. Under a new moon your bone dust becomes stardust, and there's nothing so powerful as that. (White magicians love to mix extraterrestrial bits and bobs into their charms, if they can be found.)

Set aside a tablespoon of your dust. At midnight under the new moon, scatter the rest in each of the four corners of your property, or each of the four corners of your apartment.

Place the remaining dust in the pouch and wear it as an amulet around your neck for three days; then remove it to a safe place. Never throw a filled amulet away, especially not one containing stardust! Never use it for another spell, either, and never give it to anyone else.

The Minerva
Your hairdresser's ruined your life

Based on an old Gypsy charm that's fairly harmless, the Minerva doesn't need you to come out all guns blazing. (Your hair will grow back, after all.) The Minerva does have a bit of staying power, though, because charms involving rings and circles, even knots, have the power to contain and bind enemies till you're done with them.

 You need:

+ A dollar-store, purse-sized teddy bear
+ A stitch ripper or a small pair of scissors like nail scissors
+ A dime-store rhinestone ring
+ A needle and thread

Open a seam on the body of the bear with the stitch ripper or nail scissors. Create a hole in the stuffing by taking some out if you have to. Mind you don't go all the way through the bear. Drop the ring into the cavity, pack the stuffing back in, and sew the bear back up. Take care with your stitching (think *Project Runway*). Your work shouldn't show.

Present the bear to your stylist as a good luck charm to keep at her station. If you'd rather not see her again (or if you'd rather not see anyone again so long as your hair's that charming Day-Glo green), have someone else deliver it, or simply leave it at the salon with her name on it.

From then on there'll be "just something" about her that puts her clients off.

High Pressure
Curse the weather

A simple twist on an old Irish malediction. Curse the weather by cursing the weatherman!

You need:

+ E-mail or a pen, paper, envelope, and stamp

Choose the local television weatherman who seems to give the worst forecast, either by routinely predicting good weather just to tell viewers what they want to hear, or by continually getting the forecast wrong. E-mail or snail mail him at the station with this comment: *"May every day of it be wet for ye, though not a day of it be wet for me."* Fair weather will follow for at least the next nine days.

WARNING CURSES
Snooze, You Lose

Think of them as "prevenge." Send a message or make a preemptive strike before trouble begins. (If you think it's coming, it probably is, and warning curses are the only curse type where it's best not to wait to find out.) Warning curses also ensure that promises get kept and contracts are honored.

The Four-Quarter Curse
Your partner's straying

But you can stop it! Keep in mind that it's harder to get a woman back than a man—and keep in mind that it's more often a man who wants a woman back than vice versa. So, you go, guys! Just remember, don't cut corners here. This is going to take everything you've got. And remember, too, to have a little bit of actual cash on hand for this one. While ancient curses sometimes use coins as charms and modern adaptations usually discard them, for this curse you do need a bit of change—just because you need a bit of change.

 You need:

+ A spoonful of sour milk
+ A fresh egg
+ A small potted "gift" plant, the kind you get at the supermarket (a miniature red rose is best)
+ Four quarters
+ A small gift card (free with your plant)

Don't sour the milk with vinegar; it needs to sour naturally. Just leave it out of the fridge for a day or two.

Leave the egg out as well. (Eggs represent fertility and productivity; in this case you're souring them both.)

Tip the plant out of its pot and place the egg where the plant had been. Tuck the quarters in around the egg. Replace the plant, adjusting the soil to make it fit over the egg.

"Water" with the milk and recite three times: "*Twixt he and thee is nothing more—enmity I place instead.*"

Write your partner's given name on the gift card. Tuck the card into the plant and recite three times: "*Twixt she and thee is nothing more—enmity I place instead.*"

Deliver the plant and card anonymously to the other man. Leave it on the doorstep or by a mailbox, if that's feasible; otherwise, have it delivered to his home or workplace. That's the end of that affair!

The Three-Quarter Curse
Your partner hasn't strayed ... yet

You've got only part of the problem you'd have if you
had to use the Four-Quarter Curse (p. 87) instead
of this one, the Three-Quarter. So in casting Three-
Quarter you can get away with less change ... literally. But don't rest on your laurels. (Perhaps doing
that has gotten you into this mess in the first place?)
Don't dream of cutting corners here any more than you
should if you were casting Four-Quarter.

You need:

+ All ingredients for Four-Quarters, except you need only
  three quarters here, not four
+ A dressmaker's pin
+ A few cotton balls
+ A small heart-shaped container with a lid (available from a
  dime store)

Follow directions for the Four-Quarter Curse, using
only three quarters.

After you've delivered the plant, wrap the pin in the
cotton and place it in the container. Arrange to be alone

a few minutes at bedtime for the next seven nights. Hold the container in your left hand and say: *"My lover's heart will feel this pin. Her devotion I will win. No rest for her and then no sleep until she comes to me to speak. Only when she loves me best will she find peace and, with peace, rest."*

With your left hand, place the container under your pillow and sleep with it there.

Seven nights will do the trick. Never mind that she looks like death warmed over for a week and can't stop yawning—she'll survive.

The Singularity
You have a hanger-on

The Singularity mirrors the method and the result of The Thrill is Gone (p. 102). Devised to drive away an ex-lover, it's equally good to use on any relationship that's ending—but not fast enough. It severs you from those who just won't call it a day. It's even good for driving away stalkers.

You need:
+ Two white candles
+ A match
+ Two small bowls
+ Two fresh eggs
+ A small kitchen mallet or meat tenderizer
+ A fork

Light the candles and stand them side by side on a table in front of you. Place the bowls in front of the candles. Place an egg in its shell in the bowl on the right.

Take the remaining egg and crack it gently into the bowl on the left. Say: "*My mind is gold, my body silver. My mind is single. My body is single.*"

Take the meat tenderizer or mallet and whack the egg on the right. Say: "*Your mind is gold, your body silver.*" With the fork, stir together the mess of whites, yolk, and shell, saying: "*Your mind is single. Your body is single.*"

Separate the bowls by about a foot and move the candles ahead, placing them in the space between the bowls. Say: "*Our minds are single. Our bodies are single.*"

Extinguish the candles. Rinse the intact cracked egg down the sink. Throw the smashed egg outside and cover it with a bit of earth. Wash both bowls.

The Eastwood
The curse against rude

You'll like this one lots, and you'll use it lots, too—on
people who block the aisles in the market or the stairs
in the subway; on drivers who jam up the street to wait
for a parking spot (or who steal yours); on imperious
waiters and the floor staff at Saks; on friends who
routinely take another call when you're on the line with
them; on the receptionist who chats on the phone about
what she did last night, while you wait; on chatty types
at the show, or people who leave their cell phones on . . .
(Add your rude list here. Add your whole Encyclope-
dia of Rude here.)

Today's Eastwood evolved from a type of spell used to
tongue-tie truthful (that is, harmful) witnesses in court.
But because of its potency it can bind bad behavior,
too. One of these spells, thought to be among the
oldest Sicilian spells surviving, was inscribed on a lead
"charm tablet," a totem favored by the Greeks when
they overran ancient Sicily. The tablet was round for
its type and might have been designed as an amulet,
especially because it was inscribed with mystical names

and invoked an unnamed "holy goddess." Now she'd be called Miss Manners.

You need:

+ A 3-inch paper circle
+ A pen
+ Scissors
+ Two small squares of cloth
+ A needle and thread
+ A leather shoelace

Use these materials to make a handmade, all-purpose, one-fits-most amulet, sort of like a secret decoder ring that you wear around your neck. First, in a spiral of print small enough that it all fits on, and from the outside in, write on your paper circle, "*I record my life with the holy goddess. I register with the holy goddess. She banishes the unrecorded. She banishes the unregistered.*"

Then, turn the circle over and write the same invocation, in a spiral, on the reverse.

Cut the circle along the words into a spiral, taking care not to break it. (If you do, start again from the beginning with a new circle.) Gently tease the spiral so it resists lying flat.

From your squares of cloth, make a pouch to fit the spiral. Place the spiral inside and sew the amulet shut. Rough stitching's fine; Tim Gunn won't be checking this one. Cut a small slot at the top and thread the shoelace through it.

Whenever you think you'll need it (okay, that'll be always), wear it under your clothes by tying the shoelace around your neck. Alternatively, keep it in a pocket. But don't put it in your purse or briefcase. For maximum lout protection, lodge it near your heart.

Dodge the Judge
You've been served

Fend off subpoenas and other legal papers, even a summons for jury duty. Dodge the Judge is a curse that ends things, but don't use it for evading or stopping divorce actions since curses elsewhere in this book work better at preventing romantic breakups. Don't use Judge to end a military order, either—the two spells that follow are better for that.

You need:
+ A white candle
+ A match
+ An unopened deck of playing cards

Wait for dusk, and wait for a full moon if you can. (A full moon is always the best time for stopping things.) Light the candle. Open the deck of cards. With your left hand, pull out any card to represent you, and any other card to represent the legal process you want to avoid. It doesn't matter which cards you draw at this point—though if you draw the two of spades or the four of diamonds, put them back in the deck and pick something else instead.

Set your two cards out side by side, with your card on the left.

Find and remove the two of spades from the deck. It represents togetherness.

Find and remove the four of diamonds from the deck. It represents ending.

Put the card representing the legal process in front of you, face up. Place the two of spades and then the four of diamonds on top of it, both face up as well.

Place your card on top of the other three, face down. You're on top of it all now, and facing it down.

Extinguish the candle.

Follow this procedure at dusk three nights in a row. Then replace your four cards together in the deck and store it in a safe place.

Boiled Eggs
You've been recruited

In the 1960s, there was the draft. Now, the DOD hard sell. With monthly quotas to make, today's recruiters promise signing incentives, college and veterans' benefits, safe assignments, ready opting-out. It's easy to be drawn in. But suppose you sign and change your mind? Here's help from 14th-century Scandinavia. The Vikings, arriving in Europe in 793 AD, didn't need spells—they were Vikings, after all. But the Scandinavians who survived them learned tricks from them at the same time they specialized in their own rough-hewn Norse charms. To end something resistant to ending, they buried urine-soaked eggs in ant hills. When the egg was devoured, the deed was done. You can use flat beer to get nearly the same effect, and you don't need ants or ant hills. In casting this spell, be sure to retain your original papers. Use only photocopies you've made from them.

You need:

+ A photocopy of your contract
+ A fresh egg

+ Two or so cups of flat beer
+ A saucepan

Wait for a full moon, when all cycles end before they start again. Photocopy your copy of your service contract and tear the photocopy lengthwise into long shreds.

Boil the egg in its shell in the beer, saucepan uncovered, until the beer evaporates. Cool the egg. Scrub the saucepan.

Dig a shallow hole outside and line it with the shreds of your photocopy. Nest the egg in the shreds. Cover the shallow grave with the displaced earth. Your commitment to military service is now buried.

After three days, without uncovering the egg, stamp on it until it can't help but be smashed. Cover it with more earth to prevent it being dug up by animals. Set a large rock on top. Your commitment is now destroyed.

Scrambled Eggs
You've been stop-lossed

Use Boiled Eggs (p. 98) with a variation—this time you're not hard-boiling the egg in its shell; you're cracking the egg and poaching it. It's imperative that you don't break the yolk, and sometimes even experienced cooks find this tricky. If the yolk does break at any point, discard everything and start again. (You might want to have more flat beer standing by, just in case.) As it was for Boiled Eggs, it's critical that you wait for a full moon before you perform this one. And as before, take care to retain the original copy of your paperwork.

 You need:

+ Everything you need for Boiled Eggs
+ A small saucer

In an uncovered saucepan, bring the beer to a boil. Reduce heat to simmer.

Gently crack the egg into the saucer. Slide the egg from the saucer into the saucepan; simmer for nine minutes. The yolk will be hard. Don't evaporate the beer as you would for Boiled Eggs. Instead, throw it out.

Follow the directions from Boiled Eggs.

Nine Lives Cat
Your garden's overrun by cats

You don't have to be mean about it. You don't need to upset puss or puss's owners, your neighbors. You don't even need to involve them. This is a cat curse even cat lovers can use!

You need:

+ To recall your childhood math

Stare at the cat and quietly recite the nine times table backward, beginning at nine times eleven is ninety-nine. The cat may stay until you finish, or he might leave straight away. In either case, count down to the end. Cats know the nine times table, and this cat won't be back.

The Thrill is Gone
Your love is flagging

So get it back! Here's a curse that will rejuvenate a relationship by simply scrambling a couple eggs. As always with eggs, the yolk represents the mind and the white represents the body. Mixing them up promises to bring your body and soul back into the arms of your partner.

You need:

+ A pair of red candles (don't use candles that were bought separately or don't match)
+ A small ceramic bowl (not plastic or metal)
+ Two fresh eggs
+ A fork

Light the candles and stand them side by side. Place the bowl in front of the candles and gently crack an egg into it, saying: *"My mind is gold, my body silver."*

Crack the remaining egg into the same bowl, saying: *"Your mind is gold, your body silver."*

With the fork, stir the eggs gently, breaking the yolks and mixing them together while you say: *"Our minds are gold, our bodies silver."*

When the yolks are evenly mixed through the whites, take the bowl outside and pour the eggs out in your yard. Cover lightly with a bit of soil.

BINDING CURSES
Straitjacket Your Worst Enemies

A binding curse curbs your opponent's strength. It can end stalemates, wear down enduring enemies, or simply stop someone yapping at you. Conversely, it can get you noticed and get your calls returned! Binding curses are crackerjack at breaking customer service chokeholds—everything from automated telephone answering to the bungling of your bills and subscriptions. They can even make the cable guy commit. They're also good for containing illness, or for keeping away poor health in the first place. If someone or something is oppressing you, use a binding curse.

A Separation Spell
You've been dumped—get your ex back

As curses go, returning something to the way it was is relatively easy, and most of your success here (especially whether the effect of the curse lasts) will be up to you. You're casting an ancient Greek separation spell that dates back to the late 4th century BC and kept a departed lover from taking a new one. Lovers have had their troubles for centuries, it seems, so try to lighten up about yours. The remedy here separates the lover you've lost from a new lover he or she might by now have taken on, or might take on soon. The earlier you cast it after your breakup, the better it will work. Cast it with a light and hopeful heart.

 You need:

+ A pen
+ Paper
+ A match

To get a woman back, write:

I turn away new lovers, new friends,

all others new from [your ex's name here],
from her face, her eyes, her mouth,
from her breasts, her soul, her belly,
from her groin, her back, her body,
from it all I turn them each away.
Away, away, away,
I turn her back to me.

To get a man back, write:

I turn away new lovers, new friends,
all others new from [your ex's name here],
from his face, his eyes, his mouth
from his chest, his soul, his belly,
from his groin, his back, his body
from it all I turn them each away
Away, away, away,
I turn him back to me.

Fold the paper in thirds and thirds again so you have a small square. Sleep with this square under your pillow for three nights, then remove it to a safe place.

When your ex comes back, go outside and unfold the paper, light it with a match at the bottom left corner, and scatter the ashes to the wind.

The Roundtable
You're being blackmailed

Spirits take blackmail as seriously as they do graft, so with this spell you'll be calling on your friends, the roundtable of the Spirits General, again—"the Kings, Dukes, Governors, and Commanders of the legions for the gathering of the forces to a single will." The Spirits General don't like to be summoned for small things, though, so don't cast this spell lightly.

 You'll need:

+ Paper
+ A pen
+ This symbol, for summoning them:

Draw the symbol on a slip of paper and leave it for your blackmailer anonymously: on his doorstep, in his mailbox, at his workplace. (Best not to send it by e-mail, since making your IP address untraceable is probably beyond your capabilities.)

Deliver the symbol, and that's all you have to do. The Kings, Dukes, Governors, and Commanders will take it from there. Don't forget to thank them and discharge them.

The Silencer
You're being badmouthed

No one sounds more unreliable and just plain nuts than someone spouting gibberish. That's why this ancient Roman curse, one of the oldest of its type known, kept accusers and witnesses from testifying in court by turning their words to nonsense that ridiculed them. Two small round tablets carrying the curse and dating from the early 5th century were found in a Sicilian goddess's sanctuary. One had apparently been used against a trial witness called Selinontios, the other against a second witness called Timasoi. In an effort to increase the power of the magic, the inscription on one tablet ran clockwise while on the other it ran counterclockwise. You can try that, too.

You need:
+ A 3-inch (or so) paper circle (simply trace a glass on paper with a pencil, then cut out your circle)
+ A pen

Beginning at the circle's center, print the name of the person who's slandered you. Print outwards in a spiral, repeating the name until the spiral fills the circle.

More than one person involved? Write all the names, repeating them as necessary until the circle fills. For a group, write the group's name continuously. For media, name the media outlet, and so on.

Don't know who your defamer is, just that he's out there? Write "SELINONTIOS" (the name of the first defamer this curse was used on).

Next, inscribe the flipside as above. If you don't know names, on this side write "TIMASOI" (the name of another defamer) in a spiral out to the edge.

Hold the circle, first side up, in the palm of your left hand. Say: "*I inscribe Selinontios* [or name your badmouther] *and the tongue of Selinontios* [or name your badmouther], *twisted to the point of uselessness. And I inscribe, twisted to the point of uselessness, the tongues of foreign witnesses thereto.*"

Turn it over. Say: "*I inscribe Timasoi* [or name your badmouther] *and the tongue of Timasoi* [or name your badmouther], *twisted to the point of uselessness. And I inscribe, twisted to the point of uselessness, the tongues of foreign witnesses thereto.*"

Keep the circle in a safe place. Next to your bed in your night table is good, so long as it doesn't get tangled up in junk or crushed by it. (Would now be a good time to clean that drawer out?)

Keep your circle for a year or so, just to be sure; then burn it and bury the ashes.

Debugging No. 2
You've caught a bug, No. 2

Debugging No. 2 is most often used against flus and colds. But that doesn't mean its usefulness stops there. Sorry, for the most part it's no good against ills that aren't usually caused by pathogens—headaches, for instance. (For them, try the Chopping Block, p. 143). And Debugging No. 2 certainly won't disinfect your kitchen counters! For common STDs, Debugging No. 1 (p.78) is usually your better choice. But you can try Debugging No. 2 on the bacteria that cause some stomach upsets, and even on those that cause food poisoning. Put away your Clearasil, too—you can even use Debugging No. 2 to combat acne, because bacteria is at work there. Keep in mind, though, that in the case of food poisoning you have to be quick with your curse, just because bugs that produce toxins usually do so at top speed. Just as doctors advise when it comes to taking anti-virals and even home remedies, the earlier you hit what ails you with Debugging No. 2, the more effective you'll find it at preventing illness or at least diluting it so that you'll find your recovery shortened. Unfortunately you can't use any of the three debugging curses in this book preventatively. You can't lay it (or any curse!) every day to keep from getting sick. One last and very important proviso: If you don't get better promptly, or if your condition worsens, see your doctor. Neither Debugging No. 1 nor No. 2 replaces medical advice and treatment.

You need:

+ The ingredients used in steps 2 to 5 of Pollard (p. 60).

Prepare the mint-steeped tea and the dried mint leaves as per directions 2 to 5 of Pollard.

Heat the potion to scalding; let it cool a little. Stir a teaspoon of the dried mint into a tablespoon of the tea, and drink. Make and drink a tablespoon of this mix every day for the next seven, discarding any that's left over.

The Charm Bracelet
He won't call you

Sure, the wisdom is that when a guy doesn't call within the next day or two, he'll never call. Beat the odds! Bear in mind that this curse has to be laid over the course of a month and can hardly produce immediate results. But it *will* teach you patience!

You need:

+ Three lengths of twine, each about 3 feet long
+ A red candle
+ A match

Braid the first third of the three strands of twine together in front of the lit candle on the night of the new moon. As you start and as you finish, say: "*As these knots I do entwine, let his heart be linked with mine.*" Extinguish the candle, knot your cord loosely into a circle, and sleep with it under your pillow until the middle of the month.

At mid-month, light the candle again and braid the next third, repeating the incantation as you start and as you finish. Extinguish the candle. Again tie the cord loosely into a circle, and replace it under your pillow.

Repeat the process the final time on the night of the full moon.

Sleep with the finished circle under your pillow. When he calls, remove it, burn it, and scatter the ashes outside.

Debugging No. 3
You've caught a bug, No. 3

Our final debugging curse is for the other kind of
bug: computer viruses, cookies, keystroke loggers and
the like that won't make you physically ill but that
can otherwise ruin your day. Where you cast Debugging No. 3 is crucial to ensuring its success. Tradition
has it that spells cast at crossroads are ramped up in
power and range. Crossroads can also sweep away
your ill luck. For Debugging No. 3, a crossroads is
essential, but all the same, any old crossroads will do.
The intersection of paths in a park will work, as will
a street corner. Keep in mind, though, that crossroads
curses are boosted formidably when they're cast at a
point where streams or waterways converge. Running
water is the catalyst, while standing water has the
opposite effect by stagnating energy. Try out the power
of crossroads for yourself, for Debugging No. 3 or for
any spell, and see what works.

 You need:

+ A computer memory stick, a.k.a. a flash drive

Use the flash drive you've used most recently with your desktop or your laptop. It doesn't matter what files it holds, and don't worry that they'll be destroyed or changed. They won't, though they will be cleaned, and that cleanup will migrate back into your computer when you plug the drive back into your USB port. If you don't have a flash drive, go get a new one. (You can't use one that you've borrowed, unless it's never been used.) For a new, blank drive, copy any file to it from your desktop or laptop. It doesn't matter which file you copy, and you only need one.

Take the flash drive to a crossroads and say three times: "*Go. Come.*" That's it. When you're at a crossroads, there's not much to say or do; the rest is easy.

Go home and re-attach the drive to your USB port.

Demon Mom
Your mother-in-law will be the death of you

Try a modern version of the ancient Babylonian demon bowl against her. All you need is her coffee cup, your version of the ancient "curse bowls" that were engraved with sketches of what they could achieve, sometimes along with descriptive text. A 6th- or 7th-century AD bowl dug from the banks of the Tigris pictured male demons with their hands bound and their feet chained. Get the picture? But for your mother-in-law, all you need is a mug or a cup that you've given to her specially, along with a little help from the spirit Naberius. He keeps her from speaking, except sweetly. Imagine the benefit to the entire family, even if you can never take the credit! (Never share your plans or your curse with anyone, especially your spouse.) Note that you don't have to recast the curse each time Mom visits. Once you cast it the first time, you won't want to, either.

You'll need:

+ A mug or cup
+ A pen that marks permanently on china, available from hardware stores
+ This symbol, representing the incantation of Naberius for protection and peace:

118

Three weeks before you cast your curse, buy Mom a special coffee cup and use it exclusively for her when she visits. You can always tell your incredulous spouse it's a gift to show Mom you appreciate her after all.

Sketch Naberius's symbol on the bottom of the cup with your china marker.

Bring the cup out when Mom visits; use it for her coffee or tea.

The day you cast the curse, keep the cup out of the sink once Mom empties it—no rinsing! Once she's left, make sure you're alone. Hold the cup in your right hand. With your left hand, turn it counterclockwise three times. Say: "*I charge thee Naberius, governor of nineteen legions, that thee shall hear mine command and to ignore thee shall suffer in the everlasting fire by the will and the virtue of the highest. Hear thee Naberius that the trouble wrought by another shalt be banished and not offered entrance more in that thee be bound to the pain of everlasting torment for thy disobedience. So I ask thee Naberius, so let this be done.*"

Never mind what happens next, even if nothing happens.

Wash and dry the cup and display it in a prominent place for Mom's next visit.

Discharge the spirit Naberius, with thanks.

The No-Brainer
Your boss just won't give you that raise

Really? You just haven't asked the right way. This binding spell will help. While it won't harm your boss, it will keep him from hurting you more. But first, decide: What if you don't really merit that raise? Pick up your pace in the office before you decide if you really need to cast this curse.

 You need:

+ A white candle
+ A match
+ A 12 x 12-inch square of cloth
+ A bag of cotton balls
+ A foot-long length of twine
+ A really small personal item belonging to your boss (it could be something from his desk, but even better is a hair, a nail clipping, or a thread from his clothes)
+ A needle and black thread
+ Three 6-inch lengths of red ribbon

Choose a dim room nowhere near your workplace. Part of the trick is to put some distance between you and your boss.

Light the candle.

Fashion the cloth into a poppet (see the Graverobber, p.63). Use the cotton for stuffing and the twine for securing the figure and forming a head and limbs. Sew up the seams.

Leave the head open and insert the personal item into the cavity. Sew the head shut.

To bind the figure, tie one length of ribbon around the neck; with the second, tie the arms to the torso to confine them; with the third, tie the legs together at the ankles.

Extinguish the candle.

Take the poppet outside and bury it.

Meetings
Your time is wasted at work

Is there someone officious at work you could sure do without? Your boss, perhaps, or just some little pipsqueak martinet? No doubt this control freak loves meetings, and loves to call them. Here's how to get everyone back to work.

You need:
+ About a cup of chopped mint (fresh is best, though dried will do)

Go to the boardroom or the meeting room when no one's around. If there are clocks in the room, remove their batteries.

Sprinkle the board table with mint. Circle it three times counterclockwise as you "put it to sleep" by reciting or singing this children's lullaby: *"When at night I go to sleep, fourteen angels watch do keep: Two my head are guarding, two my feet are guiding. Two are on my right hand, two are on my left hand. Two who warmly cover, two who o'er me hover. Two to whom 'tis given to guide my steps to heaven."*

Sweep up the mint and sprinkle it in the corners of the room and along the baseboards, where it won't immediately be vacuumed up. Restore the clocks.

No one will be able to stay awake in the room again, meeting keeners included.

This curse works by quieting a place, but you can try it on people, too. If the boss is a problem, sprinkle a little mint near the corner office. In small spaces you don't need much.

And remember, you can always grow a little pot of mint on your own desk.

The Vern

Your neighbor or your colleague is driving you nuts

Remember the '80s sitcom about Vern and his well-meaning nemesis neighbor, Ernest P. Worrell? "Hey Vern, it's Ernest!" While it's too late for Vern, here's a curse for you to use on that special someone you could do without. It's not terribly serious, but it will get your tormentor off your back. Use it for anyone who's a pain, but never use it against someone you envy.

You need:

+ A piece of first-quality stationery, unlined (available at a stationery store)
+ A pen
+ A few dressmakers' pins

Take your stationery and write this down: "*I give you the man who has stolen my pleasure. May the grass grow at his door and the fox nest on his hearthstone.* [Write the name here.]"

Roll up the paper and secure it with several pins. Say: "*So I give the name who took me away, who has been privy to that taking-away.*"

Place it under your neighbor's doorstep. The front step's better than the back.

For a coworker, simply place the scroll at the back of one of his least-used desk drawers. The bottom drawer on the right side is best.

When things improve, remove the roll—but keep it handy if things deteriorate again. This is not a curse with great sticking power, but it can be re-used.

The Superbowl Six-Pack
Your guy has the wrong friends

Get rid of the lot of them for once and for all, in one fell swoop, without your man ever knowing, or even suspecting, who did the deed. After all, ridding him of the "essential" relationships he's cultivated—by way of high-minded pursuits like tailgate parties or the weekly poker game—is not something he'll forgive you for very soon. Men have their priorities, after all. So beware of gloating over your success in a weak or angry moment when you want something delicious to throw in his face. Your curse will fall apart, and so will your relationship. Note: The Superbowl Six-Pack is a muscular curse, but still it can only disappear one bunch of yahoos at a time. If your guy develops a replacement clan, simply dust off the curse—and another set of glasses—and go for it one more time.

You need:

+ A match

Buy a six-pack or several as a "friendly gesture," and invite your man's friends to the house to watch the game.

Collect the beer glasses at the end of the proceedings, carefully keeping track of which glass goes with each lout.

Don't use your partner's glass.

When everyone's gone, including your partner, write all the names on small strips of paper. Drop each name into the dirty glass it goes with.

Open a fresh beer (is there one left?!) and divide it evenly among the glasses.

Set the glasses out of sight and let the beer in them evaporate. When the names are dry, dump them out of the glasses and take them outside.

Dig a shallow pit, dump in the names, and drop in a lit match. Cover the ashes with the displaced earth and fill the hole.

Run the glasses through the dishwasher on the "soiled" cycle three times.

Sweet Dreams
Her girlfriends don't like you

We know, we know: it's hard to imagine why not. But
suck it up. Your girlfriend's not going to dispatch her
friends even if you want her to. In fact, she's not going
to dispatch her friends precisely *because* you want
her to. Women have their priorities, after all. What it
amounts to is this: if you want to live with her, you're
going to have to live with them. Make the best of it
with Sweet Dreams. And remember, shouldn't any
friend of hers be a friend of yours anyway?

You need:

+ Six sheets of fine notepaper (you may have to buy a pricey
  tablet or a box, but once her friends adore you, it'll have been
  well worth it)
+ A pen
+ A straight edge

Find out the names of the women who don't like you. In
the unlikely event there are any who *do* like you, find out
their names too. Full names are best, but if you can't prod
for them without raising suspicion, given names will do.

Write all the names, pro-you and con-you, on a sheet of the pricey paper. Repeat the names across the page and repeat the block of them down the page until it's filled. Turn the page over. As above, fill the reverse side.

Take a second page and repeat these steps. (Think this is work? Want to go about trying to win her friends your way?)

With a straight edge, sharply crease 1/2-inch columns down each page. First tear one page into these columns and then tear each column crosswise into thirds. Repeat with the second page. Keep the pages separate by doing first one, then the other.

Mix up the pieces of one of the sheets by tossing them gently a few times. Lay them out flat on another piece of stationery. Cover with a second piece, and fold the stack in half and half again.

Repeat the mixing and "packaging" with the pieces from the other sheet.

Push one "package" under her side of the mattress. Push the other under yours.

Sweet dreams.

Spiders and Snakes
You have a phobia

Spiders and snakes and dogs and cats and high places and open spaces . . . Sorry, in order to cast this curse, you'll have to wait until midsummer when the ingredients you need will be at the height of their powers. They'll only disappoint if you gather them too early or too late. The ancient Celts believed that flowers picked on Midsummer's Day (June 21, the summer equinox)—and no other time—were imbued for twenty-four hours with powers more potent than any charm in the world. On any other day they were pretty and fragrant, but ordinary.

You need:

+ A 6 x 6-inch square of cloth to make an amulet
+ Cord to tie the amulet
+ Wildflowers to fill it (cultivated flowers from the florist or from your garden absolutely won't do)

Go to a forest in midsummer. If you can't manage it, you don't have to go precisely on June 21; close enough will do. If you live in a city, a romp in the forest will obviously take some planning. So plan!

Force yourself to go into the woods even if you have a spider or snake phobia, and take heart—wrigglies there are in no greater numbers than they are anywhere else, no matter what you think! Take heart, too, if your phobia happens to be agoraphobia. In the woods, you'll feel, um, snug as a bug.

Go into the woods alone. You really must. Phobias are private, not shared by most of the rest of the world, and so are spells against them.

Pick a large handful of woodland flowers. Don't dislocate entire plants or damage leaves or roots, and certainly don't take any home for your garden. It's not good karma, and it's not good ecology.

Fill your amulet while you're still in the forest; tie it up and hang it around your neck before you come out.

Wear it until the phobia leaves. Then keep it nearby for insurance.

REPUDIATION CURSES
or Curses for the Little Guy

Repudiation curses guard you from organized malice. Robin could have used them against the Sheriff of Nottingham, or David against Goliath—and how do you know they didn't? Use them against institutions (government agencies or corporations, for instance) that mislead or hurt people. Repudiation curses should not be used on a whim, and they can be like class actions: Some require group efforts and might take a while to work.

The Amen Omen
Disempowering Corporations

Consider using this curse against corporations and/or their policies. It's powerful enough to get the job done because it invokes a host of "strong angels" with a sacred incantation from ancient Egypt. The incantation is an old Coptic chant against evil, and it's full of arcane names. Do your best to pronounce them. As friends and protectors of the oppressed, the angels are on your side. Like all angels, they take themselves lightly—despite the blackguards they have to deal with, they have a great sense of humor. Still, they'd appreciate a little R-E-S-P-E-C-T, so don't mangle their names. (Pronunciations aren't given below because these names actually sound just as they look. You have to look carefully, that's all!) Respect the e-mail restrictions indicated when you cast this curse, and especially avoid "publicizing" your efforts beforehand.

 You need:

+ The following incantation
+ A bunch of like-minded friends (at least two plus yourself)
+ A private meeting place

The incantation should be delivered by a group. Enlist friends. Don't proceed without at least three of you; more is better, like a group of six, nine, twelve . . . any multiple of three.

Don't e-mail the incantation around beforehand to get a head start on rehearsing or to show how cool this spell is. Photocopy only the copies you need, and distribute them only when you gather your group. Then, as a group, rehearse the incantation until you get it right, especially the angels' names.

Once you're well-rehearsed, have the group intone the name of the corporation you want brought down, or the corporate policy. (Leave it at that. This is not the time for grandstanding.)

Then launch into the incantation, feeling the poetry and the power of the strong angels' names: "*Bael Phoel Thael Throel Thabael Thoel Bachool Thiel Aroel Afphel Arouoel Samiel Auel Ouel Ohmiel Tharimiel Achel Aaroabdel—listen to us, strong angels, for we invoke you by the Lord, you four and six and eight and all archangels of the body of Yao Yecha, that you hearken to us and send to us Athonath Athonath, that is, Gabriel, the angel of righteousness, that he come to us and do our work. Spell. Spell. Spell. Amen. Amen. Amen.*"

As you intone the three "Amens" at the end, turn slowly counterclockwise after each.

Discharge the angels with thanks.

Collect and destroy every copy of the incantation—by burning, please; no shredders. Angels love sacrificial flames. Cast the ashes to the wind.

The Indra Mantras
Bring home the troops

Hindu spells can seem daunting to cast because of their
long and foreign-sounding mantras (or invocations),
because you usually have to repeat them over a long
series of days without missing a day, and because for
solving big problems, they can take longer to work
than you'd wish. But they're among the most ancient
and powerful spells in the world. Because they're not
simple and fast, they're not used elsewhere in this
book. But for the vast and complicated problem of
war, they're who you're gonna call. (Hindu spells are
also among the classiest of spells, though they can be
used to achieve the basest of effects—keeping an enemy
from peeing, for instance!)

These Indra mantras for the troops come from the
holy Atharvaveda, a compilation of prayers and charms
selected from the Vedas. Written in Sanskrit (the
excerpts below were translated into English in 1895), the
Vedas contain ultimate knowledge. They're a "revealed"
transcription of the four most sacred, most authoritative
scriptures in India.

Following are two Atharvaveda "short" prayers you must use together in sequence every morning for twenty-one days. Mark a calendar to know where you are.

When you rise each day, collect a bit of water in a basin. Offer the first prayer, drink the water, then offer the final prayer.

The first protects the troops so long as they remain engaged. Note how comprehensive it is, deflecting even friendly fire.

The second prayer is for you at home.

Don't pray for a single soldier; pray for them all, including foreign (though not enemy) troops, and pray not just for yourself but for everyone at home. That's the way the prayers are designed and the way they'll be most effective.

These prayers are made to the gods they name, greatest of them Indra. But all those invoked must be thanked each morning and discharged, if you want them back the next morning! And then you can wake them up as early as you like.

Prayer 1, for protection from arrows and for the punishment of enemies:

Let not the piercers find them, nor let those who wound discover them.

O Indra, make the arrows fall, turned, far from them, to every side.

Turned from them let the arrows fall, those shot and those that will be shot.

Shafts of the Gods and shafts of men, strike and transfix their enemies:

Whoever treateth them as foes, be he their own or strange to them, a kinsman or a foreigner,

May Rudra with his arrows pierce and slay these enemies of theirs

The rival and non-rival, he who in his hatred curses them,

May all the deities injure him! My nearest, closest mail is prayer.

Prayer 2, to Soma, the Maruts, Mitra, and Varuna, for reversion:

May it glide harmless by in this our sacrifice, O Soma, God!

Maruts, be gracious unto us.

*Let not disaster, let not malison find us out; let not
abominable guiles discover us.*

Mitra and Varuna, ye twain, turn carefully away from us

*The deadly dart that flies to-day, the missile of the
wicked ones.*

*Ward off from this side and from that, O Varuna, the
deadly dart:*

*Give us thy great protection, turn the lethal weapon
far away.*

*A mighty Ruler thus art thou, unconquered, vanquisher
of foes,*

*Even thou whose friend is never slain, whose friend is never
overcome.*

SELF-CURSES
AND SELF-HELP
Cursing Can Begin at Home

Believe it or not, there's a use for the self-curse. It can keep you from continually missing deadlines, falling short of goals, failing to keep promises, procrastinating, overeating, drinking, or smoking. Use a self-curse as a purgative when you're sick.

The Chopping Block
You're sick

Old Norse magic to eradicate joint pains in the elderly followed the method below, except that the ancient spell used a real axe and a real woodsman. The sufferer placed first his bare right foot on the block, and then the left. The woodsman made deep cuts into the block on either side of each foot—not into the foot itself! (You were worrying about that, weren't you?) The woodsman made one chop into the block for each large joint in the body. He swung so hard (and happily, so accurately) that by the time the cure was finished, his chunk of wood was split in three. The version below is less dangerous and doesn't involve sharp edges. (And no, don't use your meat cleaver in a pinch.) Like most Norse spells, there's little chat to this one and a lot of action, but it works far better than placebo. You can use it just one time, or you can repeat it any time you get chronically ill or dragged out.

You need:

+ A chopping block or some sort of stand-in, like a chunk of wood set on its end, or a small stool (you can also simply place your foot on a step)

+ A toy hatchet

Put your bare right foot on the "chopping block." With your left hand, wave the hatchet in a counterclockwise circle over it three times. Repeat with the right hand over the left foot.

The Imbiber
Save me from myself

Know what people say about you and your bad habits?
You don't need to know. You can imagine. Overeating,
over-drinking, smoking, procrastinating, dragging
yourself in to work late every morning . . . you name
it. If you do it and you don't want to—or in the case
of something good for you, like exercise, if you *don't*
do it and *do* want to—then try salt. It's been used for
centuries to purify and to protect. Sea salt's fine. But
ordinary table salt works just as well as the artisanal
stuff you find in markets these days at a premium price.
It's true that artisanal salt has good-sized crystals, and
crystals are always useful in magic. But table salt has
crystals, too, and if you're on a budget, or if you just
want to get on with it (rather than procrastinate some
more), you can get by with the very ordinary salt box
in your very ordinary cupboard. This is a curse against
the "enemies" that defeat you, but it's also a protective
blessing for you. Unlike most spells, it could use the
occasional booster, so use the best booster days of the
year: Christmas Day and Midsummer's Day. Take a
moment on both days to repeat the spell.

You need:

+ A white candle
+ A match
+ A 1/2 cup of salt
+ A tablespoon
+ A small plate
+ A little water

This is one of the few curses for which you needn't dim the room or wait until dark. What you did in the open you can undo in the open.

Light the candle. Place the plate in front of it. Scoop two tablespoons from the 1/2 cup of salt and spoon it onto the plate. Add enough water to make a paste. Rub a little on your face and your palms. Say: "*O instruments, by fire, earth, air, and water I conjure you to banish foul creatures from me and draw all virtue to me.*"

Brush your face and hands off onto the plate. Pour the remaining salt on top. Extinguish the candle. Take the plate outside and sprinkle the salt on the ground.

BLESSING
Because It's Better to Bless Than to Curse

And because good things can happen too, and you can help them along. Use this blessing to ward off danger, and curses coming toward you and yours. Use it to protect everyone and everything you love, to help people in trouble, or to help them stay out of trouble.

The Spotted Hag
Protect persons, animals, homes, possessions, health

The charm you need is a Hindu prayer "to avert evil spirits of misfortune and to secure prosperity." It's chock-full of ghouls and goblins and fun for the entire family. So the bunch of you won't mind saying it on rising every day for the next twenty-one. (You can also cast it alone; it's just more fun if you don't have to.) Use a calendar to keep track of where you are. Consider saying it as you'd say grace at a meal; just make that meal breakfast. It's a great way to start your day! One last thing: you're invoking Hindu gods, so discharge them each day with thanks. That way, they'll return the next. Here's the prayer:

We drive away the Spotted Hag, Misfortune, and Malignity:

All blessings to our children then! We chase away Malignity.

Let Savitar, Mitra, Varuna, and Aryaman drive away Stinginess from both the hands and feet:

May Favor, granting us her bounties, drive her off. The Gods created Favor for our happiness.

Each fearful sign upon thy body, in thyself, each inauspicious mark seen in thy hair, thy face,

All this we drive away and banish with our speech. May Savitar the God graciously further thee.

Antelope-foot, and Bullock-tooth, Cow-terrifier, Vapor-form,

The Licker, and the Spotted Hag, all these we drive away from us.

CURSING FAQS

My curse didn't work. Why?

How do you know it didn't work? Leave it alone.

My curse didn't work well enough. Can I pile on more?

How do you know it didn't work well enough? Leave it alone.

I asked for the wrong result. How do I change it now?

How do you know you asked for the "wrong" result, or that you didn't get the "right" one? What part of leaving it alone don't you understand?

Someone might have cursed me. How can I tell for sure?

If someone really has cursed you, you'll know for sure. If you don't deserve it, it probably won't "take." But if you *do* deserve it, that's trickier. Use the Spotted Hag to try to escape a curse (p. 149). And best of luck!

Someone *has* cursed me. Help!

Use the Spotted Hag (p. 149). And again, good luck. Curses are easier to place than to remove.

My enemy found out I cursed him. What should I do?

Nothing. Don't brag about it, that's all. If he asks you about it, just ignore him. (But why would he ask you about it, unless you tipped him off?) If he threatens you, ignore that, too. Unless you've played fast and loose with the rules, you're safe. You cursed him, right?

How long does a curse last?

How long is a piece of string? Your curse knows how long it is. Worrying about things like this is a sign you're fussing about the outcome of the curse you cast. Don't.

I changed my mind. How do I remove my curse?

Salt purifies and protects, and so it's sometimes able to "decommission" the ingredients of a curse. Try collecting the things you used, coat them with salt—lots of salt—and burn it all to ashes in a trough in the ground. Then, bury the ashes and hope for the best. The other thing you can do is to try casting the curse again—on yourself. Be aware that nothing you try will work if you're acting out of fear, not remorse. And next time, read the label!

ABOUT THE AUTHOR

Dawn Rae Downton is the author of the memoirs *Seldom* (Arcade) and *Diamond: A Memoir of 100 Days* (McClelland and Stewart). She holds a doctorate in literature with a specialty in ancient texts, but works day to day writing news, commentary, and features for print and broadcast. She lives with her husband overlooking the Atlantic from Nova Scotia's bucolic south shore, where cursing seems neither possible nor allowed—and certainly not necessary.